Pieces Are Fun 3

Compiled, Edited and Annotated by
DAVID HIRSCHBERG

CONTENTS

Project Manager: Carole Flatau
Illustration: Lisa Mane
Art Layout: Rafael D' Sabino

LITTLE OVERTURE

THIS PIECE IS EXCELLENT FOR INTERPRETATION, TONE AND SHADING. IT IS
ALSO VALUABLE AS A STUDY IN CHORDS, FIVE FINGER GROUPS AND DOUBLE
NOTES.

CEDRIC W. LEMONT

AVALANCHE

THIS BRILLIANT LITTLE PIECE WITH ITS INTERLACING HAND PASSAGES HAS
LONG BEEN A RECITAL FAVORITE.

STEPHEN HELLER

SPINNING SONG

A MERRY LITTLE PIECE IN WHICH THE LEFT HAND PORTRAYS THE TURNING OF
A SPINNING WHEEL.   THE SYNCOPATED ACCENT WHICH CONSTANTLY RECURS
IN THE RIGHT HAND ADDS A ZESTFUL, RHYTHMIC FLAVOR.

ALBERT ELLMENREICH

MARCH

THE WORLD FAMOUS COMPOSER, PROKOFIEFF, SO WELL KNOWN FOR HIS
PETER AND THE WOLF HERE GIVES US A DELIGHTFUL PIECE FOR PIANO
STUDENTS WHICH IS IN A TRULY MODERN STYLE.

SERGE PROKOFIEFF

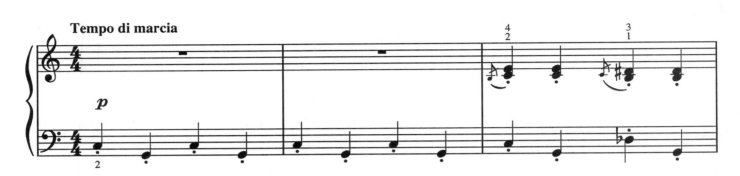

GYPSY CAMPFIRE

HERE IS A NEW COMPOSITION WHICH BIDS FAIR TO BECOME ONE OF OUR OUT-
STANDING RECITAL PIECES. IT HAS A BEAUTIFUL MELODY, RHYTHMIC COLOR,
DELIGHTFUL VARIETY AND SUSTAINED INTEREST THROUGHOUT.

LOUIS SUGARMAN

RONDO ALLA TURCA

FOR MANY YEARS THIS PIANO SOLO HAS BEEN TAUGHT BY PIANO TEACHERS
EVERYWHERE. IT IS SAFE TO SAY THAT MANY HUNDREDS OF THOUSANDS OF
COPIES HAVE BEEN SOLD OF THIS PIECE.

FREDERIC BURGMULLER

MINUET IN G

THE GRACE, CHARM AND NOBILITY OF AN OLD WORLD COURT WITH ITS
BEAUTIFULLY ROBED AND JEWELED NOBILITY SHINES THROUGH THIS ENTIRE
COMPOSITION. NO WONDER THAT THE WORLD HAS LONG TREASURED THIS
MINUET.

LUDWIG VAN BEETHOVEN

WITCHES' REVELS

THE COMPOSER OF THIS EXCELLENT PIECE HAS LONG BEEN APPRECIATED BOTH
HERE AND ABROAD AS ONE OF THE GREATEST COMPOSERS OF PIANO STUDENT
MATERIALS. THIS PIECE IS A SPLENDID EXAMPLE OF HIS GREAT TALENT AND
SKILL.

LUDVIG SCHYTTE

FUR ELISE

HERE IS A PIECE WHOSE NAME IS A HOUSEHOLD WORD. IT HAS BEEN PLAYED MILLIONS OF TIMES THROUGHOUT THE WORLD. IT STILL REMAINS LOVELY AND UNTARNISHED.

Poco moto

LUDWIG VAN BEETHOVEN

FLOWER SONG

AN EXCELLENT EXAMPLE OF THE FINE SENTIMENTAL PIECES OF YESTERYEAR.
IT STILL POSSESSES GREAT POWER TO DELIGHT AND CHARM THE WHOLE FAMILY.

GUSTAV LANGE

THE MUSIC BOX

HERE IS A PIECE THAT WILL SURELY TEST YOUR SKILL IN PLAYING SCALES AND PASSAGES. IF DONE WELL, THE BRILLIANT EFFECT OF THIS PIECE WILL DAZZLE AND DELIGHT THE LISTENER AND PLAYER ALIKE.

CARL HEINS

Allegretto e grazioso.

SONATA IN C

MOST POPULAR OF ALL THE MANY MOZART SONATAS IS THIS LITTLE GEM IN
C. IT REQUIRES BEAUTIFUL TONE, FINE CLARITY, SKILLFUL PHRASING AND
ALSO INTERPRETATION AND UNDERSTANDING OF A VERY HIGH ORDER.

MOZART

PRELUDE IN A

THE MAGIC AND SORCERY OF CHOPIN IS ILLUSTRATED IN THIS LITTLE JEWEL
FROM HIS BOOK OF PRELUDES.

FREDERIC CHOPIN

PORTRAIT OF GERSHWIN

THIS LOVELY TONE-POEM TRULY PAINTS A REMARKABLE PORTRAIT OF
GERSHWIN IN MELODY, RHYTHM AND HARMONIC VARIETY. IT SHOULD PROVE
ONE OF THE GREATEST ADDITIONS TO PIANO STUDENT'S REPERTOIRE

GEORGE BERMONT

To Richard Sheldon

Copyright 1950 by Musicord Publications, New York
International Copyright Secured

Printed in U.S.A.

ARAGONAISE

MUSIC LOVERS HAVE LONG DELIGHTED IN THIS SELECTION TAKEN FROM THE
BALLET LE CID BY MASSENET. THE STRONG RHYTHMIC BASS PATTERN HAS
SET AGAINST IT A SYNCOPATED PATTERN IN THE TREBLE CLEF WHICH IS HID-
DEN IN A SERIES OF SHORT RAPID RUNS. THE EFFECT OF THE WHOLE IS A
BURST OF MELODIC THRILLS.

JULES MASSENET

WALTZ IN BLUE

THE GREAT MELODIC CHARM AND SKILLFUL WRITING OF THIS COMPOSER IS WELL ILLUSTRATED HERE. OTHER FINE WORKS BY THIS COMPOSER ARE HIS MANHATTAN SUITE, HIS NEWSREEL SUITE AND ALSO HIS SUITE IN THREE QUARTER TIME. ALL ARE WORTHY ADDITIONS TO OUR PIANO LITERATURE.

FRANZ MITTLER

ON A MAGIC CARPET

SIT ON THIS MAGIC CARPET AND RIDE AWAY TO MAGIC LAND. BRING OUT THE
FIRST NOTE IN EACH MEASURE AND PLAY THE WHOLE COMPOSITION WITH A
LIGHT FLOWING STYLE.

CEDRIC W. LEMONT

Printed in U.S.A.

FAVORITE PIANO SOLOS
BLUE RIBBON ENCYCLOPEDIA

Rave reviews keep coming: the "Blue Ribbon" books have indeed been accorded blue ribbon status by teachers and students across the country.

✔ Music carefully selected by teacher/editor Carole Flatau
✔ Music by composers who specialize in writing for students
✔ Music with genuine pedagogical merit
✔ Music that reinforces specific concepts and keyboard skills
✔ Music of various styles in each volume
✔ Music that is good to teach
✔ MUSIC THAT STUDENTS REALLY ENJOY!!

LEVEL ONE (EL9792)

Forty titles on 72 pages, including: Beaded Moccasins (B. Frost) • Calypso Tune (J. George) • Daydreams (W. Gillock) • Doo-Dad Boogie (D.C. Glover) • Moon March (E. Pearce) • The Pleasant Peasant (J. George) • Puppet on a String (D. Karp) • Simple Soul (R. Grove) • The Trumpet Player (H. Cobb) • Two Marionettes (J.R. Poe) • Walkin' the Bass (M. Marwick).

LEVEL TWO (EL9793)

Thirty-six selections on 72 pages, including: A la Sonatina (L. Curcio) • Brown Bear Boogie (A. Kent) • Dance of the Mountain Dwarfs (F. Mittler) • The Daring Cossack (W. Noona) • I Found a Star (W. Noona) • Melody for a Monday Morning (R. Steiner) • Stroll on a Warm Day (L.F. Olson) • Sunset (C. Kraft) • Teresita (H. Cobb) • Toy Soldier Blues (M. Kahn).

LEVEL THREE (EL9794)

Thirty-three pieces on 72 pages, including: Coffee Beans (W. Noona) • Give the Bassist a Break (R. Kelley) • Glass Bells (H. Cobb) • The Hunters (D.C. Glover) • Island Song (O.N. Russell) • Jazz Miniatures (M. Nevin) • Miles of Blue (T. Caramia) • Reflections of the Moon (O. Dungan) • Rock 'n' Roll Boogie (J.W. Schaum) • Struttin' (J. Edison).

LEVEL FOUR (EL9795)

Twenty-nine songs on 76 pages, including: Chili-Sauce (H.A. Fischler) • Cool Mule (M. Kahn) • Craggy Gardens in the Spring (S.L. Dittenhaver) • Gypsy Campfire (L. Sugarman) • Jazz Prelude (M. Nevin) • Lotus Flowers in the Wind (W. Scher) • Portrait of Gershwin (G. Bermont) • Reflections in the Rain (W. Noona) • Spanish Blues (M. Kahn) • Winter Wind (G.C. Menotti).